BIBLE LEADERS WHO COPED WITH STRESS

STUDIES IN THIS SERIES *Available from your Christian bookstore*

How to Start a Neighborhood Bible Study A Guide to Discussion Study
Matthew, Book 1 Chapters 1-16
Matthew, Book 2 Chapters 17-28
Mark (recommended as first unit of study)
Luke
John, Book 1 Chapters 1-10
John, Book 2 Chapters 11-21
Acts
Romans
1 Corinthians Challenge to Maturity
2 Corinthians & Galatians A Call for Help and Freedom
Ephesians & Philemon
Philippians & Colossians Letters from Prison
The Coming of the Lord 1 & 2 Thessalonians, 2 & 3 John, Jude
Hebrews
1 & 2 Peter Letters to People in Trouble
1 John & James
They Met Jesus Eight Studies of New Testament Characters
Genesis Chapters 1-13
Four Men of God Abraham, Joseph, Moses, David
Psalms & Proverbs
Isaiah
Set Free
Courage to Cope
Promises from God
Bible Leaders Who Coped with Stress

stress

8 DISCUSSIONS FOR GROUP BIBLE STUDY

MARILYN KUNZ &
CATHERINE SCHELL

TYNDALE HOUSE
PUBLISHERS, INC.
WHEATON, ILLINOIS

First printing, December 1988
Library of Congress Catalog Card Number 88-51603
ISBN 0-8423-0375-8
Copyright 1988 by Marilyn Kunz and Catherine Schell
All rights reserved
Printed in the United States of America

contents

How to Use This Discussion Guide	7
Introduction	11
Discussion 1 *Abraham: God's Covenant Man*	13
Discussion 2 *Joseph: Man of Integrity*	17
Discussion 3 *Moses: "Why Me, Lord?"*	21
Discussion 4 *Gideon: Cautious Commander*	25
Discussion 5 *David: The Grieving King*	29
Discussion 6 *Elijah: Standing Alone*	33
Discussion 7 *Jehoshaphat: That Helpless Feeling!*	39
Discussion 8 *Jeremiah: God's Traitor*	43
Discussion 9 *Daniel: Man of Courage*	49
Discussion 10 *Esther: "If I Perish, I Perish."*	53
Discussion 11 *Ezra: Priest and Scholar*	57
Discussion 12 *Nehemiah: A Man for All Seasons*	61

HOW TO USE THIS DISCUSSION GUIDE

This study on *Stress* is suitable for use by adult discussion groups interested in the subject of stress and/or a study of Old Testament characters.

SHARING LEADERSHIP—WHY AND HOW

By using this guide an adult group will be able to rotate leadership of the discussion.

Reasons for this approach are:

(1) The discussion leader will prepare in greater depth than the average participant.

(2) The experience of leading a study enables a person to be a better participant in discussions led by others.

(3) When there is a different leader each week members tend to feel that the group belongs to everyone in it. It is not "Mr. or Mrs. Smith's Bible study."

(4) The more spiritually mature Christian with a wider knowledge of the Bible is set free to *listen* to everyone in the group in a way that is not possible when leading the discussion.

For study methods and discussion techniques, refer to the first booklet in the series, *How to Start a Neighborhood Bible Study*, as well as to the following suggestions.

HOW TO PREPARE TO PARTICIPATE IN A STUDY

(1) During the week before the group meeting, read the Bible portions listed for the next study. Read the background

passages, and then study through the sections designated for discussion.

(2) If you take a study section each day, you can cover the discussion preparation in easy stages during the week. Use it in your daily time of meditation and prayer, asking God to teach you from it.

(3) Use the guide questions as tools to dig deeper into the Scripture passages.

(4) Review the whole study before coming to the discussion. *As an alternative* to preparing daily, spend an hour or an hour and a half in sustained study once during the week, using the above suggestions.

HOW TO PREPARE TO LEAD A STUDY

(1) Follow the above suggestions on preparing to participate in a study. Pray for wisdom and the Holy Spirit's guidance.

(2) Familiarize yourself with the study guide questions until you are comfortable using them in the discussion.

(3) Try to get the movement of thought in the study so that you are able to be flexible in using the questions.

(4) Pray for the ability to guide the discussion with love and understanding.

HOW TO LEAD A STUDY

(1) Begin with a brief prayer asking God's specific help for your study together. If you find extemporaneous prayer difficult, think through and write out your prayer ahead of time. A thoughtfully written prayer asking for God's direction can be a great help to the group. You may ask another member of the group to pray if you have asked him (her) ahead of time.

(2) Read aloud the Bible portions by the sections under which questions are grouped in the study guide. It is not necessary for everyone to read aloud or for each to read an

equal amount. Assign readers by thought units (paragraphs or larger sections).

(3) Guide the group to discover what the passages say by asking the discussion questions. Use the suggestions from the next section, "How to Encourage Everyone to Participate."

(4) As the group studies the Bible portions together, encourage each person to be straightforward in his (her) responses. If you are sincere in your responses to Scripture, others will tend to be also.

(5) Occasionally a discussion will require two sessions. It is *not* recommended that you spend more than two sessions on one discussion. Each session should run from an hour to an hour and a half.

(6) Allow time at the end of the discussion to answer the summary questions, which help tie the whole study together.

(7) Bring the discussion to a close at the end of the time allotted. Close in prayer if you wish.

(8) Encourage people to *memorize* the Scripture quotation at the end of each study. If you think it appropriate, ask someone who has memorized the quotation from the previous study to repeat it for the group at the beginning of the discussion.

HOW TO ENCOURAGE EVERYONE TO PARTICIPATE

(1) It is helpful to have a number of Bible translations available in the group. Encourage people to read aloud from these different translations as appropriate in the discussion. In this study guide particular references have been made to the New International Version (NIV) and to the Revised Standard Version (RSV).

(2) Encourage discussion by asking several people to contribute answers to a question. "What do the rest of you think?" or "Is there anything else that could be added?" are ways of encouraging discussion.

(3) Be flexible and skip any questions that do not fit into the discussion as it progresses.

(4) Deal with irrelevant issues by suggesting that the purpose of your study is to discover what is *in the Bible passage* as it relates to the topic of the discussion for the day. Suggest an informal chat about tangential or controversial issues after the regular study is dismissed.

(5) Receive all contributions warmly. Never bluntly reject what anyone says, even if you think the answer is incorrect. Instead, ask in a friendly manner, "Where did you find that?" or "Is that actually what it says?" or "What do some of the rest of you think?" Allow the group to handle problems together.

(6) Be sure you as the leader don't talk too much. Redirect those questions that are asked you to the group. The leader is to act as moderator. As members of a group get to know each other better, the discussion will move more freely.

(7) Don't be afraid of pauses or silences. People need time to think about the questions and the passage. Try *never* to answer your own question—either use an alternative question or move on to another area for discussion.

(8) Watch hesitant members for an indication by facial expression or body posture that they have something to say, and then give them an encouraging nod or speak their names.

(9) Discourage overtalkative members from monopolizing the discussion by specifically directing questions to others. If necessary, speak privately to the overtalkative one about the need for discussion rather than lecture in the group, and enlist his (her) aid in encouraging all to participate.

INTRODUCTION

Think back over the difficult times in your life and the pressures you experienced. What resources did you find to help you? Although one person's stress may be another's challenge, everyone needs courage and faith to meet all that life brings.

In this study, twelve Old Testament characters experience physical, mental and emotional stress in situations surprisingly similar to those which people face today. Pressures and strains in the lives of these individuals result from varied experiences: childlessness; threats by powerful enemies; political intrigue; the approach of overwhelming military forces; disobedience and rebellion on the part of God's people; being considered a traitor because one stands alone for God; imprisonment and threat of death; constant harassment and attacks by those who oppose the work of God; perhaps most difficult of all, the rebellion and death of a much loved son.

All rational beings experience stress. Those in positions of responsibility are subject to heavier pressures and greater strain.

These studies are intended to help you:
- Learn from twelve Old Testament leaders how to cope effectively with stress.
- Learn more about the LORD as he is revealed in the experiences of these individuals.
- Apply what you learn to your life today.

Before attending the discussion group, it is important to read any assigned *background passages* as well as the sections designated for discussion.

DISCUSSION ONE
GENESIS 11:27–13:18; 15:1-7, 18; 16–18; 21:1-13; 22
ABRAHAM: GOD'S COVENANT MAN

It was probably the twentieth century before Christ when Abraham and his family left Ur, a city consecrated to the worship of the moon god. Located on the Euphrates River in Chaldea (southern Iraq), Ur was a trade center connecting the sea lanes of the Persian Gulf with caravan routes to Damascus and Egypt.

(To prepare, read Genesis 12–18; 21–22, as background before studying the passages designated for discussion using the guide questions. You may wish to discuss this study in two sessions.)

GENESIS 11:31–12:9

1. What is the LORD's command to Abram? What promises does he make (12:1-3), and what is Abram's response? Consider the stresses for those involved in such a relocation.

Share briefly if you have experienced a long-distance move.

2. Where, when, and how does the LORD's promise to Abram become more specific (verses 5-7)? What do you observe about Abram's responses to God (verses 7-9)?

GENESIS 12:10-20

3. How does Abram plan for the danger he foresees in Egypt? Describe what happens to Abram and Sarai there.

4. What action does the LORD take, and what is Pharaoh's reaction? How do you think Abram must feel at his well-deserved rebuke from Pharaoh?

GENESIS 13:1-18

5. After his chastening experience in Egypt, what significance do you see in Abram's action in verses 3-4?

6. How does Abram handle the strife over grazing space that arises between his herdsmen and Lot's? What do you learn about Abram here? What pressures does he face in this situation?

Lot is Abram's nephew and likely his assistant in managing the enlarging tribe. Their behavior as people who worship the LORD is observed by the pagan Canaanites and Perizzites around them (verse 7).

7. After Lot's choice of the more fertile land, what does the LORD say to Abram? What is his response?

GENESIS 15:1-7, 18

8. What promises does the LORD make to Abram who has no son to be his heir? Which do you think is more amazing, God's promise or Abram's response (verses 4-6)? In what situation has your faith been challenged?

GENESIS 16

9. As a film director, describe briefly how you would present the two scenes in verses 1-6 and 7-16. What stressful situation does Abram face here?

GENESIS 17:1–18:15

10. List the details of the covenant (agreement) which the LORD confirms to Abram (17:1-14). What is the significance of Abram's new name? What action on Abraham's part is the sign and seal of this covenant (verses 23-27)?

11. What startling promise does the LORD make as he changes Sarai's name? What is his answer to Abraham's desires for Ishmael?

12. What is the LORD's answer to Sarah's incredulous response to his prediction that she would bear a son in a year's time (18:10-15)?

(If you wish to handle this discussion in two sessions, plan to divide it at this point. Review briefly the first portion of the study as you begin the second discussion.)

GENESIS 18:16-33

13. What responsibility does Abraham take as the LORD reveals the likelihood of judgment upon Sodom and Gomorrah?

14. How would you summarize Abraham's reasons that the LORD should consider sparing those cities? Of what is Abraham confident (verse 25)? Why do you think he speaks of God as *judge* at this point?

15. What might be your feelings if you were Abraham pleading your case before the LORD?

GENESIS 21:1-13

16. After the miraculous fulfillment of God's promise to Abraham and Sarah, what painful choice must Abraham make?

GENESIS 22:1-19

17. Why do you think God *tests* Abraham or anyone else? What good do testings accomplish? Compare Job 23:10.

18. In what way does God test Abraham? What does the wording of the LORD's command (verse 2) reveal about Isaac's importance to Abraham? What help would it be to Abraham (and to us) to realize that the LORD understands our feelings and knows what he is asking of us?

19. Imagine what might be Abraham's thoughts, step by step, in verses 3-4. How would you paint the scene in verses

5-6? What emotions must Abraham experience through all of this, especially at Isaac's question (verse 7)?

20. What does Abraham believe (verse 8)? What does he reveal about his faith in God's promises concerning Isaac? Compare Hebrews 11:17-19.

21. At what point is Abraham's faith answered? What do Abraham and Isaac both know after this experience?

22. How is Abraham's obedience rewarded (verse 15-19)? What two reasons are given for the LORD's blessing?

Summary

1. How does Abraham handle the following stresses that he encounters throughout his life?
    - Leaving his ancestral home for a land the LORD would show him
    - Fear of physical danger in Egypt because of his wife's beauty
    - Advancing age and no heir of his own line
    - The burden of knowing impending judgment against Sodom and Gomorrah
    - The necessity to choose between Ishmael and Isaac to inherit
    - God's command to sacrifice Isaac, the one through whom all the promises are to be fulfilled

2. In what ways does the LORD help Abraham in each of these situations?

3. What have you learned from Abraham about how to handle the difficulties that life brings?

Memorize

Abraham believed the LORD, and he credited it to him as righteousness. (Genesis 15:6, NIV)

DISCUSSION TWO
GENESIS 37; 39—41; 49:33—50:26
JOSEPH: MAN OF INTEGRITY

A great-grandson of Abraham, Joseph is the eleventh of the twelve sons of Jacob (Israel). Joseph and Benjamin, born in Jacob's old age, are the only children of his favorite wife, Rachel, who died at Benjamin's birth.

(To see the life of Joseph as a whole, in your preparation for this discussion read quickly chapters 37 and 39–50. Then study through the sections designated for discussion, using the guide questions.)

GENESIS 37:1-36

1. Describe the relationships within Jacob's family as you see them in verses 1-11. How do Jacob's actions compound the family problem?

Note: Joseph's brothers saw his special robe (whether long-sleeved, vari-colored, or ornamented) as a mark of special favor, perhaps even an indication that their father intended to honor Joseph with the birthright which Reuben had forfeited (35:22; 1 Chronicles 5:1).

2. What does the fact that Joseph tells his dreams to his brothers and his father reveal about him? How do his brothers react (verses 8, 11)? What mixed feelings does his father seem to have?

3. In verses 12-28 what series of circumstances provides opportunity for Joseph's brothers to take action against him? How is his life spared?

What significance do you see in Joseph's brothers taking his robe (verses 23, 31-33)? What has it symbolized?

4. Describe Jacob's reaction to Joseph's apparent death. How do you think the brothers feel as they try to comfort their father?

5. Consider the pain that their rivalry brings to all the brothers, particularly to Reuben, Judah, and Joseph, and to their father. What do you learn from their mistakes that can help you to avoid similar ones in your family?

GENESIS 39

6. Imagine the stresses that Joseph, probably only in his late teens, must face as he enters a foreign culture as a slave. How does he fare in the house of the captain of Pharaoh's guard? Why does he succeed there (verses 2-6)?

7. What reasons are given for the complications that arise in Joseph's life (verses 6-20)? What does this chapter reveal about his character? about God's faithfulness and protection?

GENESIS 40

8. What indications do you see of Joseph's growing sensitivity to others in his position over those held in the prison? How does he honor God in his dealings with the king's cupbearer (butler) and baker?

9. What new disappointment comes to Joseph (verses 14-15, 23)? What do you imagine are his thoughts during the two years (41:1) after the cupbearer has been restored to his job? Describe your feelings when you have been cheated or forgotten.

GENESIS 41

10. Tell briefly the contents of Pharaoh's two dreams. What is his cupbearer's testimony that moves Pharaoh to call for Joseph?

How is this situation a much better time to bring Joseph to

Pharaoh's attention than an earlier opportunity the king's cupbearer might have sought?

11. Imagine Joseph's feelings as he stands before Pharaoh. What opportunities have you had to honor God as Joseph does in verse 16?

12. What is the interpretation that God reveals to Pharaoh through Joseph (verses 25-32)? What reason is given for the two forms of the same dream?

13. List the recommendations Joseph presents to Pharaoh. What does Joseph's plan reveal about his abilities to analyze and deal with a complicated situation?

14. What is Pharaoh's evaluation of Joseph? Describe the changes in Joseph's life through the king's decisions in verses 39-45.

If you were making a film, what musical background would you use for this section?

15. Note Joseph's activities as he prepares for the coming famine and then copes with it (verses 46-57). How do his sons' names reflect the changes in Joseph's life?

GENESIS 42—48

The years of famine affect all the nations around Egypt. When Joseph's brothers come to Egypt to buy grain, he recognizes them and devises a test that reveals they have changed in their attitudes. At their second visit, Joseph makes himself known to them and invites them to bring all their families and belongings with their father, Jacob, to Egypt. Presenting them to Pharaoh, Joseph arranges for them to live in the fertile section of Goshen, separate from most of Egypt. There they prosper and increase greatly in number. Before his death, Jacob pronounces God's blessings on Joseph's sons, Ephraim and Manasseh, counting them as his own sons. Thus he gives Joseph, with a double representation among the tribes of Israel, the position of firstborn.

GENESIS 49:33—50:26

16. Describe Jacob's death, and the mourning ceremonies held for him.

17. Now that their father is dead, what do Joseph's brothers fear as they return to Egypt? How do they seek to protect themselves? What does Joseph's response reveal about him?

18. What insights does Joseph have about his relationship with his brothers and the purposes God has accomplished through it (verses 18-21)?

19. What confidence does Joseph express for the future of his people, the children of Israel (Jacob)? How does he relate this to where he is ultimately to be buried?

Summary

1. List the different kinds of stressful situations that Joseph encounters throughout his life.

2. What qualities in Joseph's character do these stresses help to develop?

3. State one insight you have gained from this study that you see applicable in your own life.

Memorize

As for you, you meant evil against me; but God meant it for good, to bring it about that many people should be kept alive, as they are today. (Genesis 50:20, RSV)

DISCUSSION THREE
EXODUS 5:22—6:13; 14:1-18; 32—33
MOSES: "WHY ME, LORD?"

The family of Israel (Jacob) prospered and multiplied in Egypt, but many years after Joseph's death, under a ruler with no ties to Joseph, the Israelites became slave laborers for the Pharaoh's large construction projects. A child named Moses, born to Hebrew parents from the tribe of Levi, is adopted by a daughter of Pharaoh and raised with all the advantages of an Egyptian education. In answer to the cries of his oppressed people, the LORD sends Moses to deliver them. However, instead of letting the Israelites go, Pharaoh increases their harsh treatment.

(To prepare, read quickly Exodus chapters 5–12, 14, 24, 32–33, as background. Then study the sections designated for discussion, using the guide questions.)

EXODUS 5:22—6:13

1. Put into your own words Moses' complaint and the LORD's response in 5:22 and 6:1. How does the LORD identify himself and his concerns (verses 2-5)? What is Moses told to do?

2. What message is Moses to bring to the people of Israel (verses 6-8)? Why do you think the statement, *I am the LORD,* comes before and after the promises? How do the character and availability of the promise-giver affect the outcome of the promise?

3. Why don't the people respond to what Moses tells them? What similar situations can you think of today?

4. Imagine Moses' thoughts at the LORD's command of verse 11. How does he respond? Note Moses' and Aaron's

previous encounter with Pharaoh in 5:1-9. What types of experiences tend to undermine our ability to tackle new jobs?

5. What stress would Moses face in delivering God's message to the Israelites? to Pharaoh?

EXODUS 14:1-18

6. What reasons are given for what the people are to do in verse 1? What are the LORD's intentions regarding Pharaoh?

7. Describe the thoughts and actions of the Egyptians in verses 5-9. How do the people of Israel react to this perilous situation? What conclusions have they drawn?

8. In what way does Moses handle this test of his leadership? How does he deal with the fears of his people? What is Moses to do, and what does the LORD promise to do? What does God intend for Egypt through all of this?

EXODUS 32:1-14

As described in chapter 24, Moses has been on Mount Sinai for forty days, receiving instructions from the LORD.

9. What do the people want Aaron to do, and what reasons do they give? How does Aaron go along with them?

10. On the mountain, what offer does the LORD make to Moses when he informs him of the people's unfaithfulness? If you had been in Moses' place, what might you have been tempted to do? Why?

11. How does Moses reason with God (verses 11-14)? What questions does he ask, and what promises does he recall? How is Moses' plea answered?

EXODUS 32:21—33:6.

12. Imagine Moses' feelings as he confronts his brother and hears Aaron's excuses for failing to restrain the people. Describe Moses' actions (verses 25-29) as he deals decisively with this situation.

13. What insight do you get into the heart of Moses in verses 30-32? How does he feel about his rebellious people?

14. Describe the LORD's response to Moses' intercession (32:33-35; 33:1-3). What will the LORD do, and what will he not do?

15. List some things that you think characterize a *stiffnecked* or *stubborn* person. What psychological effect do decorative ornaments and jewelry have upon the wearer? What would their removal express?

EXODUS 33:7-23

16. Since the people have defiled the camp by their idolatry, where is the *tent of meeting* placed? How and by whom is it used (verses 7-8)?

17. What do you learn in verses 7-11 about Moses' relationship with God? How does his relationship with the LORD differ from that of the people who watch as he goes to the sacred tent? What is unique about Moses' relationship with God?

18. From the LORD's words in 32:34; 33:1-3, what is the reason for Moses' concern in 33:12, 15? Trace Moses' argument as he seeks to persuade the LORD to go with them. What is the LORD's response?

19. What do you learn about Moses' spiritual thirst from verses 13, 16, 18? What does he value? What are the things that you value? When are you most keenly aware of God's presence?

20. What will the LORD reveal to Moses (verse 19) in response to his desire to see God's glory? What experience is granted to Moses and what is denied? Why?

Summary

1. What stresses does Moses experience in the following situations?

- When he confronts Pharaoh with the LORD's command to let the Israelites go
- As he contends with his terrified people pursued by the Egyptian army
- When he comes down from Mount Sinai to find that his people have committed terrible idolatry

2. What does Moses come to value above everything else?

Memorize

Now therefore, I pray thee, if I have found favor in thy sight, show me now thy ways, that I may know thee and find favor in thy sight. (Exodus 33:13, RSV)

DISCUSSION FOUR
JUDGES 6–8
GIDEON: CAUTIOUS COMMANDER

The ancient curse, "May you live in interesting times," might well apply to Gideon. The people of Israel are being harassed by constant raids from tribes of desert nomads. Joshua and his generation have died, and the people of Israel are mixing their worship of the LORD with worship of the Baals and Asherah, fertility gods of the land.

(In preparation for this discussion, read Judges chapters 6–8 before you study the sections listed below using the guide questions.)

JUDGES 6:1-32

1. Describe the conditions in the land (verses 1-6) as if you were a newsperson reporting the events in Gideon's day. What indicates the severity of the situation?

2. When the Israelites cry to the LORD, what message does he send them (verses 7-10)? Of what past events are they reminded? Why are they now in such trouble?

3. Describe some of the "gods" that men and women serve today. How do they hinder people from worshiping the true God?

4. Ask three people to read aloud verses 11-27, taking the parts of a narrator, the angel of the LORD, and Gideon.

What is Gideon's view of the situation as he responds to the angel's initial statement? As you follow the conversation between the LORD and Gideon in verses 14-18, what do you learn about Gideon? Of what does he want to be sure?

5. Describe Gideon's experience in verses 19-24. Of what is he now convinced, and what is his immediate response?

6. What danger is involved in the assignment the LORD gives to Gideon (verses 25-27)? In what way has Gideon changed, and in what way is he still the same?

7. What are the repercussions when the townspeople discover what Gideon has done? What do they intend to do?

8. How does Joash handle this explosive situation? What challenge does he give his neighbors? What new name is Gideon called, and why?

JUDGES 6:33-40

9. Describe the emergency now facing the people of Israel. What change do you observe in Gideon, and what action does he take?

10. Of what does Gideon want to be very sure? What two proofs does he seek and receive from the LORD?

JUDGES 7

11. How do you imagine that Gideon feels when he first hears the LORD's instructions in verses 1-5? Given the chance, what percentage of the people choose to avoid the coming battle? What further test eliminates all but 300 men?

12. What reason does the LORD give for reducing Gideon's army to such a small band of men? Review God's promises to Gideon in 6:14, 16; 7:7.

13. After Gideon obeys his orders, what opportunity does the LORD give him (verses 9-15)? What does he learn that eliminates any lingering doubts and fears he may have?

14. Upon hearing the man's dream and its interpretation, what does Gideon do (verses 15-16)? What instructions does he give to his band of 300 men?

15. Describe Gideon's plan of action and the battle that follows.

JUDGES 8:1-21

16. What do you learn about Gideon's leadership abilities from how he handles the following?
    - The resentment of fellow Israelites of the tribe of Ephraim
    - The refusal of Succoth to give his troops bread
    - The remainder of the Midianite army
    - The captured kings, Zebah and Zalmunna

JUDGES 8:22-28

17. What offer does Gideon refuse? Why? Yet what action of Gideon becomes a spiritual hindrance to Israel? Why do you think Gideon the idol-breaker became an idol-maker?

How does the land benefit from Gideon's leadership (verse 28)?

Summary

1. List Gideon's strengths, abilities, and weaknesses as you have seen them in this study. Which of these do you see in yourself?

2. With what stresses does Gideon cope as he obeys the LORD's command to deliver his people from Midianite oppression?

3. What have you learned about the LORD from how he deals with Gideon? In what ways should this knowledge help you to trust God more?

Memorize

Gideon told them, "I will not rule over you, nor will my son rule over you. The LORD will rule over you" (Judges 8:23, NIV).

DISCUSSION FIVE
2 SAMUEL 12:7-23; 13; 15; 16:5-14, 20-22; 18:1—19:8
DAVID: THE GRIEVING KING

The Bible details the events of David's personal life more fully than almost any other Old Testament figure. His contribution to the spiritual well-being, comfort, and encouragement of millions around the world through his psalms make David worthy of Samuel's pronouncement, "The LORD has sought out a man after his own heart." The portions of Scripture in this study reveal a leader who gravely sinned, with severe consequences for himself, his family, and his kingdom.

2 SAMUEL 12:7-23

1. With what sins does the prophet Nathan charge David? What immediate judgment and what future consequences does the LORD predict in David's family?

2. What do you learn about David from his response to Nathan's indictment? From his actions during and after his child's illness and death?

2 SAMUEL 13

3. Review briefly the series of tragic events in this chapter. In David's time, punishment for crimes like Amnon's rape of Tamar, committed within the family, was the sole responsibility of the family and its head.

4. How do you account for David's failure to punish Amnon? Instead of facing the problem, what apparently does David do?

5. What action does Absalom take? With what results? How would David view the events of this chapter in light of Nathan's words in 12:10?

Although Absalom is allowed to return to Jerusalem (14:23-24), King David will not permit him to come to court, a clear refusal to recognize Absalom as his successor. Upon Joab's intervention, Absalom finally is received again by David (14:33).

2 SAMUEL 15

6. Describe Absalom's political tactics in verses 1-6. What is the result? After four years of wooing the affections of the northern tribes (Israel), what move does Absalom make (verses 10-12)?

7. When David learns of Absalom's conspiracy, what actions does he take (verses 13-23)? Why would he leave Jerusalem? How do his servants respond?

8. What encouragement would Ittai's commitment be to David? What is the reaction of the people who see David and his household, his soldiers and their families, going toward the desert (wilderness)?

9. What do you learn about David's relationship to the LORD from his words to Zadok, the priest (verses 25-26)? Imagine David's emotions as he sends the Ark of the Covenant back to Jerusalem and continues in his flight from Absalom (verse 30).

10. Describe David's prayer and the actions he takes as he learns that Ahithophel has joined Absalom.

2 SAMUEL 16:5-14, 20-22

11. How does David respond to Shimei's curses and stones? Why? What effect would such rejection and hatred have upon David and his group of refugees?

12. As Absalom takes over the palace in Jerusalem, what action on his part fulfills Nathan's prediction in 12:11-12?

Note: Ahithophel's advice moves Absalom to act in a way that rejects David and all he stands for.

2 SAMUEL 18:1-18

13. Contrast David's concern with that of his men in verses 1-5 as his army marches out against Absalom.

14. Describe the ensuing battle and its cost in casualties (verses 6-8).

15. You have been asked to film verses 9-17. Describe the location. Which actors would you choose for Absalom, the soldier who saw him, and Joab? Ask someone to be narrator, and ask two others to read the parts of Joab and the soldier in verses 9-18.

2 SAMUEL 18:19-33; 19:1-8

16. How must David feel as he waits for news of the battle? What conflicting loyalties and emotions would cause him stress?

17. What do you observe of David's hopes and fears as he sees the two messengers approaching? Upon learning of his army's victory, what is his first question?

18. Ask someone to interpret David's emotions by illustrating his movements and his cries of distress (verse 33). How does the king's grief for Absalom affect his whole army? Describe Joab's hard advice to David and the king's response.

Summary

1. What sources of stress in David's life are shown in this study?

2. Review briefly what you have learned about David's relationship to the LORD? Learning from David's mistakes and difficulties, what sins will you seek to avoid?

Memorize

Create in me a pure heart, O God, and renew a steadfast spirit within me. Do not cast me from your presence or take your Holy Spirit from me. Restore to me the joy of your salvation and grant me a willing spirit, to sustain me. (Psalm 51:10-12, NIV)

DISCUSSION SIX
2 KINGS 16:29-33; 17–19; 21
ELIJAH: STANDING ALONE

Upon the death of King Solomon, the kingdom split by dissension divided into the southern kingdom of Judah, which continued David's line, and the larger northern kingdom, which kept the name *Israel* under the rebel Jeroboam. Elijah exercised his ministry as prophet of the LORD about a hundred years after the time of King David in the northern kingdom of Israel during the reign of its seventh ruler, Ahab.

(You may wish to discuss this study in two sections.)

1 KINGS 16:29-33

1. What actions characterize the reign of Ahab? Into this situation comes Elijah whose name means "Jehovah is my God."

1 KINGS 17:1-16

2. How does Elijah announce himself to Ahab, and what prediction does he make?

Note: To the people of Tyre from whom Jezebel came, Baal was the sun god, or the god of storm, whose worship included bloody rites with the wild beating of drums and clanging of cymbals, prostitution, and even child sacrifice. Baal worshipers believed that he controlled the rain.

3. Where does the LORD send Elijah, and what provisions does he make for him?

Note: *Cherith (Kerith)*—east of the Jordan River, away from Ahab's capital of Samaria. *Zarephath*—near Sidon, outside the territory of Ahab.

4. What clues are given about the severity of the drought and its effects? What act of faith is Elijah asking of the widow by his request (verses 13-14)? How does she respond?

1 KINGS 17:17-24

5. Describe the emergency that arises in the home where the prophet is staying. How does Elijah handle the situation? What do you learn here about Elijah and his relationship to God? What does the widow come to believe? How would this affect you if you were Elijah?

1 KINGS 18:1-16

6. What would be Elijah's thoughts and concerns as he obeys the LORD's directive in verse 1? Imagine yourself carrying a similar message to such a person today.

7. Describe what is going on in Samaria as Elijah comes on the scene. As a devout believer in the LORD, what risks has Obadiah already taken? What does he fear will happen if he conveys Elijah's message to Ahab? What guarantee does Elijah give Obadiah?

1 KINGS 18:17-29

8. Describe the exchange of accusations between Ahab and Elijah (verses 17-19). What is the reason for the drought? What command does the prophet give to the king? Why do you think Ahab readily complies?

9. Picture the assembly on Mount Carmel. What is Elijah's challenge to the people summoned from all over Israel? Why do you think they are silent?

10. What are the rules of the contest Elijah proposes, and how do the people respond (verses 22-24)?

11. Describe the scene in verses 25-29 as if you were filming it. Imagine yourself one of those watching the contest. What effect do Elijah's taunts have upon the prophets of Baal? upon you?

1 KINGS 18:30-46

12. Note all Elijah's careful preparations in verses 30-35. What symbolism does he use in making the altar?

13. Contrast Elijah's actions and prayer with those of the prophets of Baal. What purpose for this contest is revealed in Elijah's prayer?

Note: In Ahab's day, the Phoenicians held a trading empire from Ghana to Spain and Cornwall. Israel's agricultural products traded with Tyre on the Phoenician coast brought wealth to Ahab's kingdom. Those Israelites challenged by Elijah who chose the LORD instead of Baal faced the hostility of the Phoenicians (Jezebel's people) and the possibility of commercial ruin.

14. Describe the LORD's answer to Elijah's prayer. How do the people react? What immediate action does the prophet call for?

15. Why do you think Elijah turns his attention now to King Ahab? Having demonstrated that the LORD, not Baal, is God, and remembering his declaration to Ahab in 17:1, what yet remains to be done?

16. What spiritual demands does Elijah face in verses 21-37? in verses 41-46?

(If you wish to handle this discussion in two sessions, plan to divide the study at this point. Review briefly the first portion of the study as you begin the second discussion.)

1 KINGS 19

17. Instead of honor for Elijah and the LORD of Israel, what are the repercussions in the palace of the events on Mount Carmel? Describe Elijah's reactions to Jezebel's message.

18. Why do you think that Elijah is so depressed after his great victory on Mount Carmel? What changes must he have hoped for which do not happen in Ahab? in the people?

19. What is the LORD's answer to his prayer of verse 4? What does Elijah need, and how is it provided?

20. Describe Elijah's experience in the cave at Horeb (verses 9-18). By what means does the LORD reveal himself to his servant who has been through the noise and stress of conflict with the evil of Baal worship promoted by Queen Jezebel? Compare Psalm 46:10-11.

Note: *Horeb*—Mount Sinai where God made his covenant with his people, and the nation of Israel was born.

21. What is Elijah's assessment of the situation in Israel as he answers the LORD's repeated question?

Describe a situation in which you felt like Elijah: *I, only I, am left!* How would you have to answer today if the LORD asked you, "What are you doing?"

22. What instructions and what information does the LORD give his servant (verses 15-18)?

23. Describe the call of Elisha. What stress may there be for someone like Elijah in anointing his successor?

In what situations today do Christians serving the LORD need to prepare to hand on responsibilities to others?

1 KINGS 21

24. Ask three people to read aloud verses 1-7, 8-14, and 15-16. The readers should act as if they are on a telephone party line describing what they have heard from the town gossips in Jezreel near Ahab's summer palace.

What insights do you get from the relationship between Jezebel and her husband? What role does Jezebel seem to play in Ahab's life?

Note: Leviticus 25:23 and Numbers 36:7 forbid the sale of Naboth's property.

25. Read verses 17-28 as a drama with four people taking

the different parts of a narrator, the LORD, Elijah, and Ahab.

At what point, and how, does the LORD intervene? What is his message to Ahab?

26. Surprisingly, what is Ahab's response to Elijah's severe words of judgment? With what result? How does Ahab's life affect his descendants?

Summary

1. Compare Ahab's place in history (18:18; 21:25-26) with that of Elijah's (1 Kings 17–21; Malachi 4:5-6; Matthew 17:1-13; Luke 9:30-31).

2. What kinds of stress do you observe in Elijah's life?
- In his confrontations with King Ahab
- Hiding during the long drought
- Standing alone for the LORD in the contest against the prophets of Baal
- Praying alone for an end to the drought
- When Ahab and the people fail to follow through in obedience to the LORD after the events on Mount Carmel
- When Jezebel vows to kill him

3. Describe Elijah's breakdown as a result of overwhelming stress and how the LORD heals him.

4. What have you learned from this study about how to handle stress, or perhaps how not to handle it, in your life?

Memorize

How long will you go limping with two different opinions? If the LORD is God, follow him; but if Baal, then follow him. (1 Kings 8:21, RSV)

DISCUSSION SEVEN
2 CHRONICLES 17–20
JEHOSHAPHAT: THAT HELPLESS FEELING!

During the time of Ahab and Elijah in Israel, Jehoshaphat is ruler of the southern kingdom of Judah. He inherits a kingdom strengthened by the long and peaceful reign of his father, Asa, who led his people in putting away idolatry and in turning wholeheartedly to the LORD. However, when threatened on his northern border by Israel in the last few years of his reign, Asa renewed an earlier alliance with Syria instead of depending upon the LORD for protection.

(To prepare, read through chapters 17–20 of 2 Chronicles before studying in detail the sections designated for discussion using the guide questions.)

2 CHRONICLES 17

1. What do verses 1-6 reveal about the early years of Jehoshaphat's reign regarding the following:
    - His military actions
    - The quality and direction of his spiritual life (in contrast to Ahab's—Discussion 6)
    - The results in his kingdom

2. What project does the king undertake early in his reign (verses 7-9)? What, do you think, would be the results of sending his *princes* or *officials* as well as Levites and priests to teach God's word throughout Judah? How would both people and leaders benefit from this?

3. Describe the effect of God's blessing in Judah upon Jehoshaphat's relations with surrounding kingdoms.

4. In verse 16 one of the unit commanders is identified as a man *who volunteered himself for the service of the LORD.*

What difference would such an attitude toward military service make in the morale of Jehoshaphat's soldiers?

2 CHRONICLES 18:1-4, 28-34; 19:1-4

5. When and how does Jehoshaphat become involved with King Ahab of Israel? What does he want to know before agreeing to join Ahab in battle against the Syrians?

6. Ask someone to summarize briefly the background reading of verses 5-27. In the battle what happens to Jehoshaphat? to Ahab?

7. For what is Jehoshaphat reproved, and for what is he commended by Jehu, the seer, upon his safe return home?
Note: Verse 3, *Asherah poles*—wooden poles symbolizing the Canaanite fertility god, Asherah.

2 CHRONICLES 19:5-11

8. What does Jehoshaphat set out to do throughout his kingdom (verse 4)? By what specific measures does he seek to bring peace and justice into the ordinary life of the people? What sort of persons does the king appoint as judges?

9. List the specific points Jehoshaphat makes in his charge to the civil judges in the fortified cities and to those handling civilian and religious cases in Jerusalem. To whom are they responsible?

How would recognizing these standards for judges improve the judicial system in our cities today?

2 CHRONICLES 20:1-17

10. What dangerous situation confronts Jehoshaphat in verses 1-2? What immediate action does he take?
Note: Verse 3, *Alarmed* (NIV); *Then Jehoshaphat feared* (RSV). Jehoshaphat may relate this invasion to Jehu's

declaration of the wrath of the LORD in 19:2.

11. Describe the setting in verses 3-5, 13. What is the attitude of the gathered people?

12. Ask one person to read aloud Jehoshaphat's prayer. Trace the progression of his thought in:
- How the king addresses God (verse 6)
- What he reminds God (verses 7-9)
- How he describes the current situation (verses 10-11)
- His concluding petition (verse 12)
- His realistic appraisal of their own resources (verse 12)

13. Picture yourself in a dangerous situation that is totally beyond your ability to handle. What do you learn from Jehoshaphat about how to cope with the situation?

14. Ask someone to read aloud the LORD's answer through Jahaziel. List everything the people are commanded to do. What specific promises are they given?

2 CHRONICLES 20:18-30

15. How do the king and his people react to this definite answer to their prayer?

16. Picture the scene in verses 20-21. In what way does the king exert his leadership as the people set out? How do Jehoshaphat's directions differ from those of most leaders facing such a battle?

17. How is their deliverance accomplished? Trace the element of praise throughout the situation from verses 19-28. Note: Verse 26, *Beracah* means *praise*.

18. Describe the immediate results and the long-term effects of this deliverance for the kingdom of Jehoshaphat (verses 22-30).

Summary

1. What weakness and what strengths do you see in Jehoshaphat?

2. What pressures and stress does Jehoshaphat face as a ruler whose kingdom is bordered by a larger northern neighbor, Israel (chapter 18), and is being attacked by an alliance from the east (chapter 20)?

3. *The Lord will be with you.* From this study, what have you learned about what this promise can mean?

Memorize

You will not have to fight this battle. Take up your positions; stand firm and see the deliverance the LORD will give you, O Judah and Jerusalem. Do not be afraid; do not be discouraged. Go out to face them tomorrow, and the LORD will be with you. (2 Chronicles 20:17, NIV)

DISCUSSION EIGHT
JEREMIAH 26; 36–38; 39:1–40:6; 42–43
JEREMIAH: GOD'S TRAITOR

Jeremiah lived in a dangerous place in turbulent times, for the little nation of Judah lay between the warring empires of Assyria/Babylon and Egypt. The son of a priest, Jeremiah came from the village of Anathoth, just north of Jerusalem and a few miles east of the invasion route of northern armies.

Jeremiah's prophetic ministry (627 to 586 B.C.) begins in the reformation days of King Josiah, continues through the reigns of the last four kings of Judah, and ends after the fall of Jerusalem and the exile of most of its people to Babylon.

(This study should be handled in two sessions. To prepare, read through these chapters of Jeremiah for background: 1; 26–28; 36–40; 41:16–44:30; 51:59-64. Then study in detail the passages for which discussion questions are provided.)

JEREMIAH 26

1. What message does Jeremiah receive from the LORD in verses 2-6? To whom is it directed? What is the purpose of these warnings?

Note: Verse 6, *Shiloh*—the Israelites' principal sanctuary in the time of the judges, destroyed by the Philistines about 1050 B.C. and left desolate for many centuries.

2. Imagine yourself in the place of Jeremiah in verses 7-15. Describe the response of *priests, prophets,* and *people* to the message of the LORD. Write and share newspaper headlines to summarize that day's events.

3. State the points Jeremiah makes in his defense. What hope does he hold out for the people?

4. Who takes up Jeremiah's cause? From whom and for what reasons is Jeremiah protected?

5. What light does the incident in verses 20-23 throw upon Jeremiah's words in verses 14-15? What do you learn here about his character?

JEREMIAH 36:1-7, 13-30

6. Since Jeremiah is restricted for some reason from going to the temple, what means does he use to present the LORD's message to the people? How is the time and setting of this reading appropriate to the response Jeremiah hopes for (verses 3, 6-7)?

7. Describe the reactions of the king's *officials (princes)* when Baruch reads Jeremiah's message later to them privately (verses 13-19). How accurately do they appraise the situation in the court? Compare verses 19, 25-26.

8. Picture verses 20-26 as if you were filming this scene. What does this incident reveal about King Jehoiakim and his court?

9. Imagine Jeremiah's feelings at this point. How does the LORD handle the situation (verses 27-32)?

JEREMIAH 37

10. What changes take place in Judah, and what stays the same (verses 1-2)?

11. The Babylonians withdraw their siege of Jerusalem upon hearing that the Egyptian army is marching to support Judah. Against what interpretation of these events does the LORD speak through Jeremiah?

12. How would you describe the king and the situation in the palace (verses 2-3, 11-21)? What happens to Jeremiah?

13. What kinds of stress do you see for Jeremiah in the events of this chapter?

JEREMIAH 38

14. How do the members of the king's council *(officials, princes)* view Jeremiah's message in verses 2-3? What effect do they fear it will have on the populace?

15. Jeremiah is thrown into a muddy cistern for his behavior (traitorous, as the officials see it). How is he rescued?

16. Describe Jeremiah's meeting with the king in verses 14-26. What is the LORD's answer to King Zedekiah's request for counsel? Instead of taking the decisive action Jeremiah advises, which would prevent the destruction of Jerusalem, what apparently does the king do?

17. How does Zedekiah keep his promise of verse 16 to Jeremiah (verses 24-27)?

(Plan to divide the study at this point. Review briefly the first part of the study at the beginning of the second discussion.)

JEREMIAH 39:1-14; 40:1-6

Have verses 1-10 read, one verse at a time by different people, in the style of a dirge or lament.

18. Because Zedekiah has failed to act on Jeremiah's counsel from the LORD, what happens to the king? to his family? to Jerusalem and its people?

19. What provision is made for Jeremiah by those who conquer the city? What reversal takes place in the situations of Jeremiah and of the king and his officials in chapters 38–40?

20. Try to put yourself in Jeremiah's place as he experiences these events. What mixed emotions would you have? Gedaliah is appointed governor of Judah by the king of Babylon to rule over the poor of the land who are exempted from captivity. He makes Mizpah his residence and is joined by Jeremiah and many others who have escaped the enemy. However, he is assassinated by Ishmael, a member of the royal family, and many loyal to Gedaliah are killed in the plot.

The remnant he had tried to govern, afraid of Babylonian reprisals, intends to go to Egypt for safety.

JEREMIAH 42

21. What request do the army officers and the people with them, enroute to Egypt, bring to Jeremiah? What promise do they make? How long do they wait before the LORD answers?
22. List the conditions and promises, and the commands the LORD gives in his message through Jeremiah in verses 9-12.
23. What strong warnings does Jeremiah give them against going to Egypt for food and safety? What will be the outcome for those who break their solemn promise to obey the LORD's message through Jeremiah?

JEREMIAH 43:1-7

24. Describe the reaction of the leaders of this group of refugees. Why do you think they are so vehement?
25. Who are the people that comprise the *remnant of Judah* which now enters Egypt in disobedience to the LORD?

JEREMIAH 43:8—44:30

26. Even in Egypt the LORD sends Jeremiah to speak to his people. How is Jeremiah to illustrate his message at Tahpanhes? In what way does he identify the king of Babylon? What will the LORD use him to accomplish in Egypt?
27. What explanation does the LORD give for what has happened to Jerusalem and Judah?
28. Put yourself in the position of the Jews in Egypt and try to answer each of the LORD's questions in 44:7-10.
29. List all the things in verses 11-14 that soon will happen to these people. Put this prediction in modern terms as if it were given today.
30. What explanation do these refugees see for their

experience of war and famine (verses 15-19)? What reasons do people today give for worshiping Satan, or other gods?
Note: Verses 17-19, *Queen of Heaven—Astarte,* the Canaanite goddess of fertility, love, and war. Before the reformation led by King Josiah, the people had worshiped this idol in the prosperous time of Manasseh who had encouraged them in idolatry.

31. In contrast to their ideas, what reasons (verses 20-23) does Jeremiah give for the disasters that have come upon them?

32. Ask one person to read verses 24-30 forcefully and dramatically. Ask other members of your group to describe their feelings and fears as they listen to Jeremiah's words.

Summary

1. Summarize Jeremiah's experiences as the prophet of the LORD, noting:
    - The content of his messages
    - The place in which he speaks
    - His audiences
    - The differing reactions to his messages
    - How he is treated

2. Imagine yourself in Jeremiah's place during his long ministry. What stresses would these experiences bring to you?

3. How does the LORD provide for his servant? What do you learn about the character of God as he is revealed in Jeremiah's messages?

Memorize

Thus says the LORD: *"Let not the wise man glory in his wisdom, let not the mighty man glory in his might, let not the rich man glory in his riches; but let him who glories glory in this, that he understands and knows me, that I am the* LORD *who practice steadfast love, justice, and righteousness in the earth; for in these things I delight, says the* LORD.*"* (Jeremiah 9:23-24, RSV)

DISCUSSION NINE
DANIEL 1; 2:10-30, 46-49; 6; 9:1-19
DANIEL: MAN OF COURAGE

After Nebuchadnezzar of Babylon broke the power of Egypt in 605 B.C. at the battle of Carchemish, he attacked Jerusalem where Jehoiakim, son of Josiah, ruled as a vassal of Egypt. Daniel and his friends are among those taken as captives to Babylon at this time. Less than twenty years later the entire city of Jerusalem is destroyed and most of the population of Judea deported to Babylon.

(If you are not familiar with the life of Daniel, read chapters 1–6 and chapter 9 as background in your preparation for this study.)

DANIEL 1

1. What do you learn about Daniel from the qualifications the king of Babylon specifies for those chosen for training as officials in the royal court? What provisions does the king make for these youths?

2. What problem does Daniel see with these provisions (verse 8)? How does God help him to handle the situation? With what result (verses 15-16)?

Note: The king's food probably had been offered to idols, making anyone who ate it a participant in idol worship. Also, meats would not be prepared in the ways required by the law of Moses.

3. What gifts and abilities are you aware of in your life? Compare yours with those that God gives Daniel and his three companions.

4. Describe their "final exam." How do these four young men rank in the testing?

DANIEL 2:10-30, 46-49

5. Troubled by a dream that he either cannot or will not relate to his advisers, Nebuchadnezzar asks that they tell him the meaning of his dream. How do they respond to his demand? What reaction does this bring from the king?

6. What do you learn about Daniel from the way in which he handles this dangerous situation (verses 13-18)?

7. Outline Daniel's prayer in verses 20-23 as he responds to God's answer. How does he describe God's abilities and actions? Who does he acknowledge that God is?

8. Describe the conversation in verses 24-30 between Daniel and the king. What clear witness does Daniel give on behalf of his God (verses 27-30)? When have you had an opportunity to bear witness to the God of Daniel?

9. As a result of this situation, what honors come to Daniel and to his friends?

DANIEL 6

10. By now Daniel is over eighty, and Babylon has fallen to the Medes and Persians. What changes take place under the new ruler, and how does Daniel fare?

11. Read verses 3-5 in at least two translations. What abilities and what qualities of character does Daniel evidence? Could verses 4-5 be said of you?

12. Describe the tactics that the *administrators (presidents)* and *satraps* use against Daniel. How does Daniel respond to the situation (verses 10-11, 13)?

13. What warning for leaders do you see in Darius's experience? How have Daniel's enemies trapped the king?

Describe the different ways that Daniel and the king spend the night (verses 16-18).

14. Compare verse 23 with Psalm 118:8-9 and Isaiah 12:2. In what situations in your life have you learned to trust in God?

15. Contrast Daniel's experience with that of his enemies (verses 22, 24, 28).

16. What does King Darius's decree reveal he has learned about the God of Daniel?

DANIEL 9:1-19

17. From his study of Jeremiah's writings, Daniel learns that Babylon's domination over Judah is to last seventy years (see Jer. 25:11-12). Recognizing that this period soon will be over, what action does Daniel take?

18. Follow the line of thought through Daniel's prayer. As he identifies with his people, what does Daniel confess? What does he acknowledge about the calamities that have come upon Judah and Jerusalem? What does he request of the LORD?

Note: The answer to Daniel's prayer is brought by the angel Gabriel (verses 20-23), the same messenger sent many years later to announce to Mary that she will be the mother of the Messiah.

Summary

1. Describe the different kinds of tests and pressures which Daniel experiences in his long life:
    - As a young Jewish exile in the pagan court at Babylon
    - As a member of the group of wise men threatened with death if he does not interpret the king's dream
    - As the victim of a plot by jealous colleagues intended to cause his death
    - As a person concerned for the deliverance of his people from exile

2. How would you describe the LORD as you see him revealed in Daniel's life and experiences?

Memorize

We do not present our supplications before thee on the ground of our righteousness, but on the ground of thy great mercy. (Daniel 9:18, RSV)

DISCUSSION TEN
ESTHER 1–4; 8:1-17
ESTHER: "IF I PERISH, I PERISH."

Cyrus, who conquered Babylon in the time of Daniel, built the vast Persian Empire, and his successor, Darius, organized its administration. He was followed by Xerxes (with whom Ahasuerus of this book is usually identified). The story of Esther takes place in the winter capital of Susa in Persia.

(In preparation for this discussion, plan to read through the whole Book of Esther, at one sitting if possible. Then study the sections chosen for discussion using these guide questions. In addition, someone should be prepared to summarize the events of chapters 5–7.)

ESTHER 1

1. Look at a present day map for an idea of the extent of Ahasuerus's empire (verse 1). What variety of people would be present at the festivities in verses 2-8?

2. Describe the setting and the table service of the banquet that culminates the six months' display of Ahasuerus's wealth to delegates gathered from all over his vast empire (verses 4-9).

Note: Persian customs of that time did not prevent wives from dining with their husbands. The number of people involved likely made it necessary to have a separate banquet for the women guests.

3. What connection do you see between the timing and the nature of the king's command in verses 10-11? Although no explanation is given for the queen's refusal to come, what possible reasons can you suggest?

4. Infuriated by Vashti's refusal, whose counsel does the king seek? What ramifications does Memucan foresee? What action is taken to placate king and nobles? Describe the results hoped for.

ESTHER 2

5. What plans are suggested for replacing Vashti with a new queen? How are Mordecai and Esther drawn into these events?

Note: There is a period of about four years between Vashti's removal and the search for a replacement (1:3; 2:16). It was probably during this time that Xerxes mounted a campaign against the Greeks in which he was defeated.

6. What is the background of Mordecai and Esther? Describe Esther and what happens as she is brought to the king's palace. What is the usual procedure for those who come into the harem of the king?

Note: Verse 5, *Jew*. From the time of the exile, the term was used to designate any Israelite, even though the word was derived from *Judah*.

7. What aspects of Esther's behavior do you think lead to her becoming queen (verses 7, 9, 15-17)? Whose advice does she take?

8. What insight do you get into the relationship between Esther and her cousin Mordecai (verses 7, 10-11, 20, 22)? How does this connection save the king's life?

ESTHER 3

9. Trace the events that lead to Haman's plan to destroy the Jewish people. What possible clue is given as to why Mordecai continues to refuse to kneel down to Haman (verses 2-4)?

10. If Mordecai rejects the king's command as demanding worship for Haman (which would be idolatry), what behavior can be expected of all the Jews? Should this be the case, how

would this explain Haman's intention to take vengeance on all the Jews?

Note: Because the Persian Empire extends through most of the areas in which the Jews are scattered at this time, such a program of destruction could very well wipe them off the earth.

11. What clever phrasing does Haman use in the accusations he makes in his appeal to the king, and what monetary payment does he offer?

12. Once he has the king's signet ring, what action does Haman take? Describe how you would present verse 15 in three short vignettes.

ESTHER 4

13. How do Mordecai and the Jews in every province react to the king's edict? What detailed information does Hathach bring to Esther from Mordecai?

14. What does Mordecai want of Esther, and how does she reply? Read aloud Mordecai's answer to Esther (verses 13-14) and her response (verse 16).

15. Describe the various kinds of stress there would be in this situation for Esther.

ESTHER 5-7

16. Ask one person to summarize the events of chapter 5, another those of chapter 6, and a third the events of chapter 7.

ESTHER 8

17. Even though Esther is given Haman's estate and Mordecai becomes second in rank to King Xerxes, all Jews, including Esther and Mordecai, remain in peril of their lives.

What initiative does Esther now take on behalf of her people? How does the new edict written by Mordecai in the king's name counteract that previously sent out by Haman? What is the outcome of Esther's actions?

Note: The Jewish feast of Purim celebrated today commemorates the deliverance of the Jews through Esther's courage.

Summary

1. Consider the stress that the following situations must have brought into Esther's life:
    - The early death of her parents
    - Her removal from Mordecai's home to the king's harem
    - Being made queen in Vashti's place
    - Mordecai's plea for her to intercede with the king on behalf of the Jewish people
    - Approaching the king and facing Haman, the enemy of her people
    - Pursuing the matter until Haman is dead and the Jews are delivered

2. Although God is not mentioned by name in the Book of Esther, what evidence do you see of his overruling in human affairs on behalf of his exiled people?

Memorize

For if you keep silence at such a time as this, relief and deliverance will rise for the Jews from another quarter, but you and your father's house will perish. And who knows whether you have not come to the kingdom for such a time as this? (Esther 4:14, RSV)

DISCUSSION ELEVEN
EZRA 7; 8:15-36; 9; 10:1-17
EZRA: PRIEST AND SCHOLAR

Almost seventy years after Judah came under the Babylonian Empire, Cyrus the Persian conquered Babylon and issued a decree allowing the people of Judah to return home with the gold and silver vessels captured from the temple in Jerusalem. A group of exiles returned to their land, the temple was rebuilt and dedicated in 516 B.C., and the worship of the LORD was restored in Jerusalem (events described in Ezra 1–6). It is nearly sixty years after that when Ezra is sent to Judah (Ezra 7). Esther's story takes place during the time between the rebuilding of the temple and Ezra's return to Jerusalem.

EZRA 7

1. What do you learn about Ezra's background, his character, training, and abilities (verses 1-11)?

2. To what three goals has Ezra devoted his life (verse 10)? What do you observe about the progression of these goals? What happens if a leader attempts to reverse their order? What goals characterize the spiritual leaders you have known?

3. Observe carefully the document King Artaxerxes gives to Ezra in answer to his requests. What permission is granted, and what assignments is Ezra given? From what sources will Ezra obtain the provisions he needs?

4. What do verses 21-24 reveal about Artaxerxes' theology, and his understanding of the God whom Ezra serves? What do people know about God from you?

5. In addition to his responsibilities for investigating Jewish observance of the law of God (verse 14), what other assignment and authority is Ezra given (verses 25-26)?

6. For what blessings does Ezra praise God?

EZRA 8:15-36

7. Outline Ezra's activities in verses 15-20 and 24-30. What is Ezra's charge to the twelve leading priests? How should this affect the way in which they view their responsibilities (verses 28-29)?

8. What insight can Ezra's charge to the priests give concerning the way that those who serve God today should fulfill their responsibilities?

9. How do you relate to Ezra's problem in verses 21-23 and his decision on how to handle it? People sometimes speak of having heavy responsibilities. How does Ezra face his?

Note: Ezra and his company must travel some nine hundred miles up the Euphrates River and across country to enter Judah from the north. They will carry a valuable cargo, so this decision is not taken lightly.

10. Imagine the emotions of those returning with Ezra from exile. How does Ezra describe their journey and their activities upon arrival in Jerusalem?

11. What dangers would be avoided by Ezra's actions in verses 25, 33-34? How might this serve as an example for anyone doing the Lord's work today?

EZRA 9

12. Before Ezra has time to obey the emperor's command in 7:14, what troubling situation is brought to his attention by some of the leaders in Judah? Who are the chief offenders?

What similar examples of faithless behavior are there today on the part of some who are supposed to be spiritual leaders?

13. How does Ezra express his grief at what he hears? Who joins him in his concern and mourning?

14. Ask one person to read aloud the prayer in verses 6-15 while the others listen as if they are among those present in Jerusalem in Ezra's day. Though he himself is not guilty, why do you think Ezra identifies himself with the people's guilt and shame?

15. How does Ezra describe the sins of his people? What does he acknowledge about their defeats in battle and their exile? What explanation does he see for their return to the land?

16. After all of these experiences, what disobedience have the people repeated? How seriously does Ezra view this matter (verses 14-15)?

EZRA 10:1-17

17. What effect does Ezra's public weeping and prayer of confession have upon the people? How does Shecaniah express the intentions of the people (verses 2-4)? What do they want now of Ezra?

18. What continues to characterize Ezra's mood even while he takes action on what the people have agreed to do?

19. List the steps Ezra takes in verses 7-17. What actions does he call for by those who have married foreign wives? Why would such drastic action be necessary for this nation newly restored to its ancestral land (9:1-2, 7, 14; 10:10)?

Summary

1. Describe the kinds of stress that Ezra faces when:
   - He has to decide whether or not to ask for soldiers and cavalry to protect his caravan on their journey to Jerusalem
   - He has made the decision to ask only for God's protection

- He has responsibility for overseeing the treasures being returned to the temple in Jerusalem
- He faces a situation in which many Jewish men (including leaders and officials) have married foreign wives contrary to God's clear commands.

2. Compare your own concern for obedience to the law of God with Ezra's concern.

Memorize

For Ezra had set his heart to study the law of the LORD, and to do it, and to teach his statutes and ordinances in Israel. (Ezra 7:10, RSV)

DISCUSSION TWELVE
NEHEMIAH 1–2; 4; 6:1–7:3; 12:27–13:31
NEHEMIAH: A MAN FOR ALL SEASONS

During the thirteen years since Ezra's mission to Jerusalem, local opposition has sabotaged much of the work of the city's restoration. Artaxerxes is still the ruler of the Persian Empire.

(To prepare, read quickly through the Book of Nehemiah before concentrating your study on the sections designated for discussion. It will not be possible to read aloud all the sections to be discussed, so it is important that everyone prepare in advance.)

NEHEMIAH 1

1. What disturbing news is brought to Nehemiah by his brother and others arriving from Judah? Describe Nehemiah's reaction.

2. Trace the elements of worship, confession, and petition in Nehemiah's prayer. For what reasons does he expect his prayer to be answered (verses 8-10)?

NEHEMIAH 2

3. Describe the opportunity which Nehemiah uses four months later to speak to the king about his concern for Jerusalem. What prayerful planning and administrative ability is evident in Nehemiah's request? How does the king respond?

4. How would the task of rebuilding Jerusalem compare to Nehemiah's secure position in the Persian capital? What costs are involved for him?

5. After handing the king's letters to the governors of the *province Beyond the River (West-of-Euphrates Province,* TEV), Nehemiah proceeds to Jerusalem (verses 9-11). What does he do before speaking to anyone about his plans for the city? How do the people (verses 16-18) respond to his evaluation of the situation and his report of God's help to this point?

6. Describe the opposition (verses 10, 19) and how Nehemiah handles it.

NEHEMIAH 4

7. As the repair of the walls proceeds (described in chapter 3), how do Sanballat, Tobiah, and their men react? What tactics do they employ to discourage the builders (verses 1-3, 7-11)?

Note: Sanballat, governor of Samaria, is revealed in secular records of the time to be a man accustomed to subservience, flattery, and bribes from his neighbors.

8. Describe the reactions of Nehemiah and the people of Judah in verses 4-6, 9.

9. What further problems arise (verses 10-12)? List the practical steps that Nehemiah takes to meet the difficulties and fears of the people in verses 13-23? What physical and spiritual leadership does Nehemiah exert?

10. How do you think that you would respond to such leadership if you were one of these builders? Imagine you are one of the men under Nehemiah. Relate this experience as if telling it years later to your grandchildren.

NEHEMIAH 5

Division arises between rich and poor, hindering the work of rebuilding the walls. Because of famine, the poor of the land are having to borrow money from the wealthier members of the returned community, and the lenders are requiring interest and security in the form of property and even their children. Nehemiah asks the lenders to return the property and people, appealing to his own example as governor. Though entitled to financial support by the people of the land, Nehemiah has never asked this and has borne the heavy expenses of his large household himself.

NEHEMIAH 6:1–7:3

11. Since ridicule, show of force, threats, and internal discontent have not stopped the building of the city walls, what new tactics do the enemies of this project use (verses 1-13)?

12. How does Nehemiah deal with each of these schemes? What do you learn about him from his prayers in verses 9b, 14?

Note: Verse 5, *an unsealed letter*. To leave a letter unsealed in that day was a deliberate way to make certain its contents would be publicized.

13. What effect does the success of Nehemiah's project have on surrounding nations? Though the completed walls prevent attack by outside enemies, what problem continues to plague Nehemiah (verses 17-19)?

14. What steps does Nehemiah take to make sure that life in the city will be peaceful and orderly?

NEHEMIAH 12:27-47

15. Imagine that you are to organize preparations for the dedication of the wall of Jerusalem. Describe the arrangements in verses 27-30, 31-39, 44-47. What do you learn here about Nehemiah's abilities?

16. Describe the dedication ceremonies and the emotions of everyone participating (verses 40-43). How must Nehemiah feel, remembering his solitary nighttime journey of

inspection two months before in contrast to this joyful procession of choirs?

NEHEMIAH 13

17. What actions are taken in Judah in response to the Book of Moses (verses 1-9)?
Note: *Tobiah* was an Ammonite (2:10).

18. Summarize briefly the additional reforms that Nehemiah finds necessary in verses 10-13, 15-22, 23-30? To express his frame of mind, read aloud Nehemiah's prayers in verses 14, 22b, 29.

Summary

1. Describe the kinds of stress Nehemiah faces when he:
   - Hears of the sad condition of Jerusalem and its people
   - Presents his petition to the ruler of the Persian Empire
   - Sees for himself the condition of the walls of Jerusalem
   - Faces the continued organized opposition of neighboring people who do not want Jerusalem to be rebuilt
   - Returns from reporting to the king to find that Tobiah has a room in the temple and the house of God neglected
   - Finds that the Sabbath is not being honored
   - Discovers that men of Judah are marrying women of neighboring pagan peoples

2. Upon what resources does Nehemiah depend to face these situations? What do you learn from him about how to handle such difficulties? What is the ruling concern of Nehemiah's life?

Memorize

O Lord, let your ear be attentive to the prayer of this your servant and to the prayer of your servants who delight in revering your name. Give your servant success today by granting him favor in the presence of this man. (Nehemiah 1:11, NIV)

NOTES

NOTES

NOTES

NOTES

NOTES

NOTES

NOTES

NOTES

NOTES

NOTES

RECOMMENDED PROGRAMS
FOR SMALL GROUP DISCUSSION BIBLE STUDY

New Groups and Outreach Groups
- Mark (recommended as first unit of study)
- Acts
- John, Book 1 (Chapters 1–10)
- John, Book 2 (Chapters 11–21)
- Romans
- Four Men of God (Abraham, Joseph, Moses, David)
- 1 and 2 Peter (Letters to People in Trouble)
- Genesis (Chapters 1–13)

Groups Reaching People from Non-Christian Cultures
- Genesis (Chapters 1–13)
- Mark
- Romans
- Four Men of God (Abraham, Joseph, Moses, David)
- Philippians and Colossians (Letters from Prison)

Church Groups
- Genesis (Chapters 1–13)
- Matthew, Book 1 (Chapters 1–16)
- Matthew, Book 2 (Chapters 17–28)
- 1 Corinthians (Challenge to Maturity)
- 2 Corinthians and Galatians (A Call for Help and Freedom)
- 1 and 2 Peter (Letters to People in Trouble)
- Psalms and Proverbs
- Four Men of God (Abraham, Joseph, Moses, David)
- Bible Leaders Who Coped with Stress
- Isaiah

Mission Concerns Groups
- Luke
- Acts
- Ephesians and Philemon
- The Coming of the Lord (1 and 2 Thessalonians, 2 and 3 John, Jude)
- Romans
- 1 John and James

Advanced Groups
- Courage to Cope
- They Met Jesus (Eight Studies of New Testament Characters)
- Hebrews
- The Coming of the Lord (1 and 2 Thessalonians, 2 and 3 John, Jude)
- Promises from God

Sunday School (Adult and older teens)
- Matthew, Book 1 (Chapters 1–16)
- Matthew, Book 2 (Chapters 17–28)
- They Met Jesus (Eight Studies of New Testament Characters)
- Courage to Cope
- Set Free

Biweekly or Monthly Groups
- They Met Jesus (Eight Studies of New Testament Characters)
- Set Free
- Courage to Cope
- Psalms and Proverbs

How to Start a Neighborhood Bible Study (A Guide to Discussion Study) is also available.

IF

—you have found this study worthwhile
—your group is interested in being in touch with others involved in Neighborhood Bible Studies
—you would be willing to have NBS put people in touch with you who move to your area from other parts of the country and wish to find a new group
—your area or church would like to sponsor an NBS seminar
—you would like to hear what other groups are doing
—you would like to share what has been happening in your Bible study group

LET US HEAR FROM YOU!

....

QUESTIONNAIRE

1. Our Bible study group has met together for _____ years.
2. There are _____ (number) people in our group.
3. Our group is made up of (men, women, men and women, couples).
4. We are a (neighborhood, office, church, _____) group.
   Describe something about your group: _____
   _____
5. We meet _____ (how often) at _____ (place).
6. _____ percent of our group are studying the Bible for the first time as adults.
7. We have studied the following books of the Bible using NBS guides:
   _____ .
8. The best method for adding new people to our group has been
   _____ .

   _____ other group(s) have started from our group.
9. We take turns being the discussion leader for the week, increasing participation and learning. (yes) (no)
10. Additional comments: _____
    _____
    _____

(Clip and send. You may use label below.)

....

To:
NEIGHBORHOOD BIBLE STUDIES, INC.
Dobbs Ferry, New York 10522-0222